How to Create Passive Income:

Including 5 Ideas
That Worked For Me

FRANK MERRICK

ISBN: 9781794603301
ISBN-13:

DEDICATION

To everyone brave enough to step out of mediocrity
and live the life of their dreams!

CONTENTS

Acknowledgments   i

Introduction: What is Passive Income?   1

Chapter 1: Traits of Successful Passive Income Earners   Pg 5

Chapter 2: The Untold Truth About Passive Income   Pg 8

Chapter 3: Top Passive Income Sources   Pg 11

Income Source No.1: Kindle Self-Publishing   Pg 12

Income Source No.2: Amazon FBA   Pg 21

Income Source No.3: Niche Websites   Pg 27

Income Source No.4: Dividend Investing   Pg 35

Income Source No.5: Peer-To-Peer Lending   Pg 38

Epilogue   Pg 41

ACKNOWLEDGMENTS

I am grateful to everyone with whom I had the pleasure
of working with throughout this project.

INTRODUCTION:
WHAT IS PASSIVE INCOME?

Just imagine:
-Income while you sleep
-Income while you eat
-Profit while you walk the dog and see your friends
-Cash flow while you relax on the beach

These are some of the notions people have about passive income, and they are completely false. If you started reading this book with the purpose of making these fantasies and fallacies come true, then stop reading right here. This book is for people who genuinely want to put in the effort to create passive income streams, and know that their contribution in life will be equal to their output.

But in order for you to understand this book, and how important it contents might be for your financial future, you first need to understand what passive income is. A passive income source is one that is received on a regular basis, but one that won't require regular effort to maintain.

This doesn't mean you wouldn't have to put substantial effort into it. Just as a rocket uses more fuel during the first few minutes after lift-off than it does over the days and weeks that follow when it covers more than a million miles, you will have to, at the beginning, put more effort than most people do in their regular jobs, but after the initial work and risk-taking, you will keep getting a regular income indefinitely.

Many people who have heard the term "passive income" on Instagram or other social networks assume it is something where you work for some days, and just sit back and count your millions. Such people are bound to fail, because they aren't willing to put in the work, and don't have the courage to take the necessary risk involved.

Passive income, in the coming years, will be very important for your financial well-being. The cost of living continues to go in an upward curve year after year, and our incomes aren't keeping up with them. Many of us need multiple jobs just to keep afloat. But, one thing doesn't change for anyone, from the richest of the richest, the 0.001% to the 1%, to the poorest of the poorest: time.

Everybody has 24 hours in a day. No matter how rich you get, you cannot buy time. You can't get 25 or 26 hours. 24 hours, that's it. That's all you get. So even if we manage to work multiple jobs, eventually time becomes a limit and relaxation is compromised, to the detriment of our health and relationships. Sure, working harder and longer will usually guarantee more income, but you'll soon begin asking questions.

Is it worth it?
How far do I have to go until my back-breaking hard work begins to outweigh my benefits?

While dedication and hard work is commendable, nowadays it has become common. This is the reason why you should look for other paths, where your time is dedicated to building a money-making machine for you, thus finally paying off your hard work.

If you look at all the self-made millionaires and billionaires out there, you will always see that they had their priorities right. They invested their hard work in building a business and a money-making machine for themselves, rather than investing countless hours into a dead-end job never destined to go too far.

Everybody works hard, working hard is easy, but during the rain, while all birds find shelter under the trees, the eagle flies above the clouds. Problems are the same, attitude is what makes the difference.
This book will help you make a huge difference in your life by helping you build passive income streams, of course, it won't be quick. You'll have to be patient, but before you know it you'll have several passive income streams coming at you, making you rich without having to work 100-

hour weeks.

There are many different types of income sources that could be classified as passive income. Some examples are:

-Any income that you make off your property. This could include rent from apartments, several units, or even your home; farming; or leasing out your land.

-Earnings that you might get from a business where you are not directly involved as the owner. You might own the business, but someone else is running it and taking care of its day-to-day running.

-The interest that you make from your bank account. Usually, this is not high enough to be taxable because you will be lucky if you make a few dollars from the transaction. There are a few banks that offer higher rates and if you invest wisely, it is possible to make more.

-Royalties, in the form of patents, a book, a software product, or other intellectual and creative property. If you write a book, and it becomes a bestseller, you make a high income from it for a long time, but you're not out there in the bookstores actually selling it. You just wrote it once, and then everything else is done for you, while you just keep earning the money and doing whatever you want to do.

-Interest from things like bonds and stocks.

Any of these can be considered passive income, but these were just some examples, we'll look at many others in detail later on. But from these, you can understand that it's not easy to create a big passive income source, you need expertise in some way and you need to learn. For example, the royalty checks from a bestselling book are an amazing thing, but writing one is equally nightmarish. And you can make a good income from rental properties, but you have to worry about filling the buildings, cleaning them, and going around and purchasing new properties if you would like to have more income. It is possible for everyone to make a passive income, but not all are suited for the hard work, persistence, risk-taking, and patience needed for it.

Many people who attempt to earn a passive income find that they fail with it because they are just not prepared to do the work or invest the money. They think that just a little bit of their time will be sufficient in order to get the money that they deserve so that they can go sailing around the world and live the life of the rich and famous. While this is a nice little dream, it really is not a reality.

The people who make a good living on passive income are the ones who are willing and ready to put in the hard work that is required. They are not the ones who sit back and expect the money to just be handed to them, and they are not the ones who will be duped into giving up all of their money by flashing lights and a lot of big words on a webpage. They are the ones who can think outside the box to the bigger picture, who will put in the work, and who will take the chances that no one else is willing to take in order to make a good income. They are also the ones who realize that they are never going to be able to take a break from their work, but that the reward, as well as the freedom, are so worth it.

Theoretically, anyone could be like this, but the truth is that most people are either not hard enough workers, have trouble thinking critically, or just do not have the ambition to get the work done in order to reach their goals.

To be successful in this you not only need to know the technical details and expertise, but also the traits of successful people. If you can apply them to your life, you will become rich, and get any amount of income you want.

This book will teach you everything, but you would need to have an open mind. Abandon all your negative and limiting beliefs, about how you cannot make a big income, and how you will most likely fail. You have a great amount of power inside you ready to be shown to the world, but negative beliefs are holding you back. How can you break free? Turn your negative thinking inside-out. Instead of thinking, "how you cannot make a big income?" think "I deserve to earn a big income." Instead of thinking, "I will most likely fail," think, "I am destined to win!"

CHAPTER 1:
TRAITS OF SUCCESSFUL PASSIVE INCOME EARNERS

Now that you know a little about passive income, it should be interesting to learn about people who are actually successful with it. I've been a passive income earner for a long time. I make money from Amazon Kindle, from Udemy, my blogs, email marketing and even Amazon FBA (we'll learn about them later on). I failed many times, but once I put in the work, and got going, it became easy. You have to be addicted to the results. The thing is, I've been fortunate to have a career where I can meet and work with some amazing people from all around the world, and for some time now, I've been noticing some common traits in these individuals, who are in good health, are making a huge income and are genuinely happy with their lives. So these are some traits, that, if you apply to your life, will guarantee that you will succeed in making a huge passive income stream. Don't neglect this chapter based on the fact that it doesn't have technical information.

This is just as important.

1. Persistence, Patience and Hard Work

Successful people understand that without hard work you get nowhere in life. They know the basic science of life: your input will equal your output. They don't depend on luck to get them anywhere, they depend on their skills and ambition to get them to where they want.

They have sacrificed everything to get to their position and will eat and sleep thinking about work. It becomes a part of their life and even if they have to stay up for a few days or be up at 5 am every morning, they make sure they do it because they love it.

They will rarely complain about how hard they are working because they know that all their hard work will pay off. They expect the utmost from themselves - and when they are focused, there is nothing that can stop them.

2. Easy is Boring

Many people I have worked with want to be challenged in life. They love a challenge that will test their desire to succeed to its limits. They don't want to do easy things, because they know doing something easy is wasting your time because you aren't moving forward. When you challenge yourself and keep going on until you succeed, you come out stronger and wiser from the other side.

3. Network = Net Worth

Your network is your net worth, as the good old saying goes. I've always noticed that the people who can generate a high passive income are constantly networking with others, exchanging information and asking people what they do before they even ask their name. Successful people have a Rolodex full of people who value their friendship and return their calls. In today's world, it is all about the people you know and how they help you get to where you want to be.

4. Go-Getters

Successful passive income earners are go-getters. They don't just sit back and let things happen for them. They write down goals, work towards them and achieve them. Earning this kind of income is sometimes scary at the beginning for a lot of people because it is not always guaranteed. Many people might not like working for a boss they do not like, but they do like the predictability that comes with going to work each day and bringing home a reliable paycheck that can help support their family. This is not something that can be promised with a passive income. This is a part of the tradeoff. Yes, you have to give up some of the predictability that you love with your regular income, but with some hard work you might be able to bring in a lot more money than you would from your old job, plus you get to be your own boss. There might be a lot of strange hours, but you would have more control over them and could make it to the big games or the concerts that you used to miss due to work.

5. Passion

You have to love what you are doing and the freedom that it can give you if you are looking to be someone who is successful at passive income generation. Anyone who is looking to be an entrepreneur is going to be really passionate about the things that they are doing and this is a big reason that they are so successful in their work. When you are passionate about something, you are more likely to work hard at it. You want to see how far you can take it and you will always be able to find something new and exciting that will draw you towards the work again. Those who are working with streams of passive income are going to have a lot of the same passions as other entrepreneurs since they will also be striking out on their own. The passion is the thing that is going to keep you moving forward, even when things get a little rough, you lose a little money, or when the work is not always that much fun. You can apply this trait of top passive income earners into your life by choosing a passive income source to work on that you are passionate about, and would do even if you weren't being paid for it.

CHAPTER 2:

THE UNTOLD TRUTH ABOUT PASSIVE INCOME

The thing about passive income is that sometimes it's not all that passive. Let's take real estate, for example. I still remember the late-night infomercials of Carlton Sheets when I was growing up in the 80s. The promise of easy cash from an empire of rental houses made Carlton rich, but the same can't be said about the people that plunked down hundreds for his course. My own experience with passive income from real estate will help to prove the point.

The housing bubble was inflating spectacularly. I had always been interested in investing and completed an 18-month internship as a commercial real estate analyst. I put down $33,000 to buy my first house.

The addiction was instantaneous.

I rehabbed the property and refinanced to cash out everything I had in it plus a few grand. The tenant rent was paying the mortgage and I moved on to buy my second rental.

Then I bought a third…and a fourth. I bought five single-family properties and a duplex within three years of starting in rental real estate.

The problems didn't take long to surface. My real estate empire wasn't yet large enough to become a full-time income. The rents covered the mortgages with a little left to pay for maintenance but not enough to cover my own living expenses or enough to pay a property manager.

That meant, while it wasn't a full-time income, it was getting to be a full-time job.

It didn't take long for it to become too much trying to juggle my day-job in corporate finance with nights and weekends managing my rental properties. I started to let tenants slack on the rent because I didn't want to start eviction procedures and then have to rehab the house to get it back on the market. Cash flow suffered, and I started dipping into savings to pay mortgages.

What followed was financial ruin and two important lessons about passive income.

1. It can take time before an investment becomes passive income. Real estate rentals can provide passive income but that's only after building the business to a point where you can outsource management.

2. Never confuse an investment or a business as a passive income source. I love investing in stocks, but they aren't passive investments, you had to work to make that money in the first place. Similarly, starting your own business can be a great source of wealth but nobody will ever care about your business as you do. That means you'll always have to watch management and put in some work.

The Ugly Truth

Whenever you look at a passive income idea, understand there will probably be a trade-off in the actual amount of passive income it produces and the work you put in. For example, a lot of people consider dividend stocks as a passive income source. Investing in a company that pays a quarterly dividend certainly meets the standard of no effort on your part. You'll receive those dividends every three months and won't have to lift a finger.

On the other hand, you're not going to get rich on dividends. The average payout for stocks in the S&P 500 is under 2% a year. That means a dividend of just $20 for every $1,000 you have invested. That's beside the fact that you had to put in the work to earn that $1,000 in the first place.

One of the most important personal finance books I've read is Rich Dad Poor Dad, and from it, the lessons I have learned have become part of my life. What I learned from it is that one of the habits of the wealthy is investing in assets. It's this habit of buying assets, investments that produce cash flow, that makes the rich 'richer' while the poor are spending all their money on liabilities. The rich buy an investment in a video game maker, the poor buy an Xbox that requires them to spend even more money on new games every month. While I love my passive income assets and

it's one of the top ways the rich use to grow their wealth, understand that there are a lot of myths and outright lies out there about passive income though. Even with the best sources, you'll either need to put in the work to create an asset or the ongoing effort to build it to the point you can pay for management. Stick with it though and you'll have an asset that generates cash well after you've stopped working.

CHAPTER 3:
TOP PASSIVE INCOME SOURCES

Pat yourself on the back. Making it this far in the book is a great achievement. You read all the harsh truths about passive income but still persisted, and cleared all the myths in your head about it. You have a desire to be your own boss, and do what your heart desires, while getting richer every day on the side. And now is the time you have been waiting for. You have learned a lot about passive income, now you're about to get your hands dirty and get technical.

So, are you ready? Let's begin.

INCOME SOURCE NO.1:
KINDLE SELF-PUBLISHING

If you don't know, Kindle Direct Publishing is a platform where you can self publish your books for free. Kindle direct publishing, or KDP, is Amazon's self-publishing platform where you can easily publish your own books, maintaining complete control over them while at the same time reaching out to millions and millions of readers worldwide.

It opens up the writing market like never before. Whatever your target field may be, from novels to manuals, there is virtually no limit to potential success. With Amazon's far-stretching and global reach, audiences worldwide can quickly be introduced to your content.

The aforementioned control over your content is one of the key benefits of this system. What this means is that any editing, formatting, covers, etc. are up to you, and you only, to guide and organize the way you see fit.

With Kindle direct publishing, you can earn royalties on your work of as much as 70% of the cover price of your books. KDP also gives you the ability to publish quickly, making your books available on the Kindle Store within a few hours or even minutes upon uploading of your material.

Can you imagine how unbelievable this would have been a couple of decades ago, or even more recently? There is nothing stopping you from publishing a book within minutes, for millions to have instant access to! I mean, getting your work published, let alone making it so available, used to be a real headache for writers. Well, that time is gone.

KDP gives you the opportunity to market your books to millions and millions of readers worldwide with the presence of Amazon.com in practically all countries. Lastly, KDP allows you to make your

books available for everyone as eBooks that can be read through Kindle devices and free Kindle apps while caring for the environment. Self-publishing, as a means of passive income, is becoming even more popular these days. There are a couple of reasons for this. First, most of the obstacles or entry barriers that normally face new businesses aren't in self-publishing. What they mean by this is to self publish your own books on Kindle, you don't need specialized software, you don't need to be an authority figure, expert or guru in a particular which you like to write on, you don't need to do network marketing or connected influencers, you don't even need to sell to people directly or address or market, and you don't need to spend a whole lot of money. In fact, it is possible to earn from Kindle self-publishing without having to spend anything more than the cost of your Internet connection.

As a matter of fact, not even substandard quality of your written content will necessarily preclude you from making money off it. Certainly, you should always dedicate your best efforts to producing quality, but this may not be the actual determining factor in particular niches or specific target audiences. Depending on the field you want to traverse, your potential readers may care more about the gist of the writing, rather than academic prowess or lingual expertise.

The fact that it is so simple to get into self-publishing on Kindle also means much less risk, or rather, the freedom to take more risks than you could in the traditional publishing world. This is because these platforms are not very demanding investment-wise and allow much more room for experimentation and trying out different niches, approaches, and styles. Another reason for the rising popularity of self-publishing is that it provides a very good opportunity to earn a good passive income. It is one of my favorite passive income sources. I've published 50 books in the personal finance niche and make $1000 a month from each. I spend about $20 a month in advertising for each book but do almost nothing else to sell the books through Amazon.

It's about as close to passive income as I've found but each book still takes considerable work to create. I spend upwards of 60 – 80 hours writing each book and an average of $500 in expenses from cover design to editing. The book launch is another week of work and only then does the book have the momentum to be truly passive. But after all the work is done and you've written your bestselling book and uploaded it to Amazon.com's Kindle Store, you can relax and wait for sales to trickle in.

Lastly, this can give you a huge opportunity for achieving fame and good income. Considering that Amazon is present in practically all countries all over the world in the millions of people who buy books on the Kindle Store, you have a sea of opportunities for success.

The Process:

Researching the Book

The first step to successfully self-publishing your first Kindle eBook is to do your research. The odds of successfully publishing your first, as well as your subsequent, eBooks on the Kindle Store depends highly on your ability to know the right niche or topics to cover.

Many self-publishers make the potentially fatal mistake of assuming that topics they are very much interested or passionate about or topics that they strongly feel will be ahead will make for very good topics to self publish books on. Now I'm not saying that such topics are doomed to failure automatically. While it's good if you can publish on something that you are very interested or passionate about, there's more to successfully self-publishing a book then writing on such topics.

The key to determining if a potential niche will be profitable in self-publishing is to choose topics that many people are interested in. By researching first on what people want, you practically eliminate the chance of failing on your first self-publishing attempt. This is because you will be self-publishing based on a model that has worked for all businesses since time immemorial - supply and demand.

So when doing your research, it is important to look for patterns in the place where you will be selling your self published eBooks - the Amazon Kindle Store. So what is it specifically that you should look for in terms of patterns?

First, look at the different books that cover or focus on the same topic or niche. Next, evaluate the positions of these and other similar books within the context of the overall sales of the Kindle store as well as the top 100 best sellers in their categories. Lastly, look for a marketplace or niche that is not yet crowded because those are the ones you have a significantly higher chance of dominating and succeeding in.

If it is possible to reconcile that which is in demand with the content you really want to write, then that's even better. However, the market may often dictate that you completely abandon certain ideas and force you to adapt to the supply-demand dynamics of the market.

Now, this is just the start. As much as you can significantly increase the chances of successfully publishing your first eBook on the Kindle Store — and by successfully I mean earn income - it's not a guarantee. You'll next need to come up with a good book that's worth your market's time and money. And the first thing you'll need to do in order to do that, regardless if you'll be the one to write the book yourself or hire someone else to do it, is…

Outlining the Book

Creating an outline for your self published eBook can go a long way in helping you write one that is very easy to read as well as understand. Nothing else can sabotage your self published eBook more than being scattered and unorganized. By creating a good outline, you minimize the risk of coming up with an eBook of poor quality and significantly increase your chances of self-publishing a high-quality one. Outlining also makes it much easier for you to write your eBook.

So how do you go about creating a very good outline for your first self published eBook? For starters, you can start with the table of contents of the books you evaluated earlier. The beautiful thing with Amazon's Kindle Store is that it allows you to take a sneak peek inside the books it sells. You can check out those books' tables of content so that you can have an idea of what it is you need to cover for your particular topic. It can also give you an idea, if you are well versed on the topic or have done enough research for it, of what else is missing from most of these books so that you can cover them in yours.

The review section is another useful resource for creating your outline. Consider both the negative and positive reviews, but pay more attention to the negative ones. Negative reviews give you important insights as to the weaknesses of books that have been published on the same niche or topic ahead of you that you can fill in or exploit. Essentially, negative reviews can help you avoid pitfalls that can sabotage your outline but don't look for the 1-star ones, they are highly one-sided and have no insight. Look for the 3-star ones. They have a lot of insight in them and have the reviewer generally writes what could've been improved by the writer in it. Knowing that you can pick up from where that writer left off.

Positive reviews give you insights into what other books have done right, what your potential readers will appreciate best and of course, what ideas to further build on. You don't necessarily have to reinvent the wheel but you can make the existing wheel much better and succeed in self-publishing your first eBook on the Kindle Store.

Finally, after the groundwork has been laid down through sufficient research, and an idea of the demands has been clarified by looking at reviews, it is time to move on to the main work.

Writing The Book

Now that you have created your outline, it's time to write the book. You can do this in two ways: hire a ghost-writer or write it yourself. If finding time to actually write a book, good writing skills, and expertise on a certain topic or niche are serious challenges for you, then hiring a ghost-writer is the way to go. No, I'm not talking about hiring Casper the Friendly Ghost or some other spooky elements to do the writing for you but people who can actually write well on your chosen niche or topics and are willing to transfer all rights to the written work to you. In other words, ghost-writers are people who are willing to write your book for you and give all credits due, financial and otherwise, to you in exchange for a fixed pay. You'll publish the book under your name and get all the glory, fame and most importantly, royalties.

So where can you hire ghost-writers who'll do the dirty work for you? There are many websites you can check out such as Upwork formerly known as an Odesk, Elance, and Freelancer.com, among others. Hiring ghost-writers is very easy. The challenge lies in hiring good ones. You will have to do due diligence and maybe even ask for legitimate samples of their work in order for you to screen out the good writers from the bad ones.

One way you can have an idea of whether or not a prospective ghost-writer is good is by looking at their profiles' client feedback section. There, you can see how their past clients feel about the quality of their work. In the same section, you can get an idea of their average rating.

Another way to get an idea of a perspective ghostwriters' caliber is by checking out how long have they been writing or working for clients in the website as well as how many gigs they worked on already if such information is possible or available. It's a good way to gauge how much writing experience they already have.

Keep in mind that quality always comes at a price. As such, prospective writers that charge rates that are ridiculously low - compared to most other ones at least - may be having a hard time getting enough clients to make a living one way or the other. While it's not a guarantee of poor writing skills, chances are theirs may not be of high enough quality or that they don't have enough experience yet. Either way, it's your choice and risk.

The more prominent freelance websites, such as Upwork for example, can help you attract the breed of writer most fitting for your budget. While setting up your project, it is possible to provide specifics concerning your situation and resources. The level of experience you are looking for or are able to pay for can be presented in the description. What this means is that you can point out that you're willing to accept less experience, but for less pay, and vice versa. This serves to better illustrate your conditions and needs to all potential writers.

Granted that with buying these services comes risk, follow the steps mentioned above and that risk becomes minimal.

Making the Cover and Title

Two very critical aspects of your eBook are the title and cover. While it's true that it's what's inside that counts, your cover and title are the ones that will entice potential readers to at least check out the content by either "looking" inside or downloading a sample. These two are the doors through which people need to enter in order to see your book's content. If the door's unattractive, they won't even consider peeking inside.

Both your cover and title must stand out and be different, i.e., eye-catching. Given that the average prospect on Kindle has limited time to choose and tons of other books to sort through, they'll most probably pour over the available books on Kindle quickly and as such, your book only has a second — probably even a split second — to convince readers to interrupt their searching to check out your book's contents or descriptions.

Contrary to traditional wisdom, people will indeed judge a book by its cover, and they'll judge it quickly and ostensibly. Given that your eBook has quality content, the cover and the title are definitely that which will captivate and pull in the vast majority of your potential readers.

Whatever one tries to sell in life, the importance of visual appeal can never be neglected. Not only is the initial appeal essential, but, it can prove very advantageous.
Many things have been sold solely on first glance, often regardless of the inner values! That, of course, doesn't mean that you should sell nicely packaged but horrible content, after all, in the writer's market, you have to mind feedback.

The best way to create a great cover is to get professional help. Fortunately, it doesn't cost much to get great book covers done these days. You can outsource from websites like Fiverr, where all gigs are standardly priced at $5.00. The important thing is you already have an idea of what you'd like the cover to be about so the graphic artist can easily do the cover per your specifications. If not, it may take a little bit of time and going back-and-forth to get right.

Once you get the cover done, it's time to work on your title. Your title gives readers an idea of what your book is all about in just a couple of seconds. This is where great copywriting comes into play. Good copywriting can help you relay to your potential buyers what your book's about, which will be the main criteria by which they'll decide whether or not to buy your book.

Some good tips to make your title stand out and grab the readers' attention and convince them to at least check out your book's Amazon page and sample include:

-The title must identify the main benefit of reading the book like weight loss or better health, for example;
-The title must be specified in terms of benefits identified like "Increase Sales by 100% in 1 month."; and
-The title must be keyword rich so that it will rank well in searches for certain keywords in Amazon, because the first step for getting noticed is being seen and if your book doesn't rank well in Amazon searches for your niche's or topic's keywords, the probability of it being seen is very low if not nil, after which it will end up in the "KDP Graveyard" of forgotten eBooks. You don't want your book to end up there.

If wordplay is not your strong suit, it is again possible to employ the services of a freelancer, a copywriter, who has a very strong grip on magically arranging words. For a minimal investment, you will equip your book with an effective title, which may subsequently prove crucial in capitalizing on your work. I have witnessed clients setting up projects and contests on freelance websites, looking for copywriters to brainstorm on their company name or slogan in exchange for a prize or a small fee.

Description

Your book's description can make or break your book's success. While the cover and title entice people to take a peek at your book, your book description is what can give them a clear picture of what to expect from your book. It's what can give readers that strong push towards checking your book out further by downloading a sample of it and checking out the reviews if any.

This is also the part where there is room for creativity and clever writing, but don't ever lose sight of your goal - pulling in the customers! Relative to the theme or genre of your book, different tactics may apply to spark interest - among readers. If the book is a work of creative storytelling, perhaps a thriller element may work well in your description. On the other hand, if it is a more instructive/educational piece, it may be a good idea to keep very clearly to the point and core of the content. Given that consumers are hasty and usually impatient in their searches, it may also be important to remain concise, as most people can't be bothered to read a long and vague description.

Your book's description is practically your main sales page and as such, it's a great idea to learn some copywriting techniques and principles to increase its chances of enticing readers to buy your book or download a sample at the very least. Do it well and you'll be able to convince people to buy your book. Do it poorly, then your book ends up in the dreaded "KDP Graveyard."

Price

People want to get the most value for their money. While it's true that content is what ultimately gives people value for their money, people still want to get such value at a certain price. Lamborghini makes the best cars in the world, but not everyone buys them because obviously not a lot of people have sufficient money to buy it! You might think your book offers a lot of value and is great fun to read, but the price is important to people and so, it is paramount that you optimize your price well, especially in the beginning. Once you start selling, your income, as well as your feedback, will tell you if the price can be increased or must be decreased.

Regardless, you should make every effort to get it right at the very start in order to maximize your performance on the market.

So what's the ideal price for your eBooks? The first consideration is the market. Most Kindle eBooks are priced between $0.99 and $2.99 for an eBook that's about 10,000 - 15,000 words on average so you may want to price somewhere in that range.

Another good way to price your books is by considering those of similar books in your niche or market, especially the best-selling ones. This should give you an idea of what the market may think the value of your eBook will be. Looking at the competition and paying close attention to the way they do things is always profitable. When it comes to prices, the average pricing in your field should be well understood and explored. This will show you where and how you can take advantage. Sometimes, taking your price a little under that of the competitors might just give you the edge you need. At the same time, if you know you've got premium content then this information will tell you just how far you can take it and not overprice your product. Another consideration is your desired royalty income. Pricing your eBooks between $2.99 to $9.99 gives you a royalty income of 70% of the price per unit of sales while pricing it outside that range - higher or lower - reduces it to just 35%. For maximum royalty income, the sweet spot, therefore, is the $2.99 to $9.99 range.

Publishing The Book

Now that your book is done, and all the missing pieces of the puzzle are in place, the last frontier is to simply publish it on Amazon's Kindle Store. The writers of the past would have thought you had lost your mind if you told them that, in the future, there will be a marketplace where publishing is actually the easiest step! Just follow the instructions on the website, which are pretty easy to follow, and wait for it be approved and available for purchase at the Kindle Store. It's that easy!

Promote

While it's not entirely necessary, promoting your book can significantly help boost sales. You have several options available both paid and free. You can always use your social media accounts like Facebook and Twitter to promote your book for free. For paid alternatives, you can use Facebook advertisements as well as outsource it via websites like Fiverr.com, among others.

I've encountered a lot of failure in this marketplace, before making it big and securing a high, regular income, but don't worry, if you follow these tips, you will have a much safer (and awesome) journey!

INCOME SOURCE NO.2:

AMAZON FBA

Amazon FBA - or Fulfilled by Amazon - is a program that lets you sell your goods on Amazon's online store. Fulfillment of orders is possibly the biggest challenge facing many online entrepreneurs but with FBA, it's a breeze. You can simply store your products in Amazon, who'll be the one to take care of the logistical stuff such as warehousing, shipping to buyers, handling after-sales concerns and provide great customer service. This frees up a lot of your time to focus on what really matters - providing great, value-for-money products to customers.

Just consider how much you can improve and consolidate your business venture if you are unburdened of the most demanding tasks at hand, which as I've stated are usually the logistics.

The new vacancy in your schedule will provide ample time for the procurement of products and expanding the variety of your assortment, setting up relationships with quality suppliers, etc.

Needless to say, this is an obvious and enormous advantage from the very get-go when compared to other means of online sales. It is incredible to realize that we live in a time where a small business, as small as a hobby even, can simply sign up and begin cooperating with a conglomerate that is Amazon. And not only cooperate, but directly reap the benefits of their powerful establishment to advance your own income.

Another thing worth mentioning is the fact that this system will serve you just as well if your goals are not all that high. What I mean by this is that FBA can also be used to simply liberate yourself, aiming to spend the free time on things other than your online business. Once you have established a satisfactory amount of consistent income from your sales, you may want to just lay back for the most part and let the money dribble in, turning your income into truly passive income.

As mentioned before, most of the required management or intervention in your business can be automated or delegated to other people. In the course of building your passive income system on FBA, you'll see for yourself the ways in which your specific operation can become more and more autonomous.

AMAZON FBA VS. AN ONLINE STORE

Aside from who's handling the logistical stuff, there are other reasons why Amazon FBA is superior to setting up and managing your own online store. First is faster delivery. With Amazon's extensive market reach and logistical capabilities, it doesn't take long for your stuff to get to your customers. Contrast this with doing the shipping yourself. Not only will this help to better satisfy your customers, but fast shipping also expands the array of products you can sell. Time-sensitive goods which may expire, or otherwise suffer due to prolonged shipping processes, are one such example. Quick shipments, with a guarantee of such an enormous enterprise, are an advantage hardly earned when you're out there by yourself.

Second, FBA gives your products significantly more exposure than if you'd promote it on your own. It's because Amazon is the biggest online retailer in the world — even bigger than most other physical retailers! By having your products on Amazon FBA, you enjoy much higher visibility and potentially, significantly more sales than if you'd do it in your own online store. Of course, complete independence may have an appeal, but setting up shop and making a name for yourself may take years upon years of hard work and commitment.

Apart from being exhausting, the risks and possibilities of failure if you're going it alone are substantially higher. Seeing as you are reading a book on passive income, you probably aren't very enthusiastic about the whole prospect of putting years of work into a venture that may not even pay itself off.

Third, making your products available on Amazon's FBA allows your customers to avail of its free shipping within 2 days and other similar delivery options. Again, this is a logistical advantage you can leverage to sell more of your products efficiently. Furthermore, this and other advantages offered to customers on Amazon are one of the reasons that this platform enjoys such a wide consumer base throughout the globe. This is exactly how this universally beneficial system operates in a way that provides all parties their slice of the cake.

Lastly, FBA gives you - as an online seller - much-needed credibility because simply put, Amazon is one of the most trusted brands in the world.

Can you imagine how beneficial it is to piggyback on the reputation of one such as Amazon? Lovely, isn't it? This brings us back to the subject of making a name for yourself as an online retailer, as this step of the way is pretty much not an issue on FBA. Naturally, you still want you to get positive feedback and ensure a satisfied customer base, but the degree in which FBA facilitates this process for you is truly invaluable. Should any issues arise after the shipment, Amazon's highly professional staff will handle their end in customer services and any potential complaints or misgivings. As far as buyers are concerned, they are dealing primarily with Amazon, while you come into play as a third party that offers the products, and is vouched for by the renowned Amazon Company.

Seeing up your FBA Business

It's not rocket science to set up your own FBA business and start earning passive income. It'll take some work, though. As is the case with most other passive income sources, it's all about building a solid foundation for your FBA business. Here are the steps towards enjoying passive income via Amazon FBA:

-Account: Sign up for a professional account to maximize seller benefits.
-Niche: Research what niche is best to get into and generate ideas on what products to sell on FBA. Some niches are definitely profitable while others are trash so research well. This means some quality market study and analysis until you get a good grasp of the supply-demand climate in a particular niche, as well as the nature of the competition therein.

-Suppliers: After determining what particular niche and products to sell on FBA, you'll need to find a good supplier. A good supplier is one that doesn't just provide quality products but also delivers on time - ahead of schedule even. When looking for the right supplier, consider asking for samples, determining a good lead-time and estimate your potential margins on the products.

-Listing: Once you've found a great supplier, you should make a listing for your chosen product on FBA. Use good keywords and great content to make your product page the best that it can be. Popular keywords and Search Engine Optimized descriptive content often play a big role in attracting potential customers. Again, if SEO writing and handling keywords successfully are tasks you find difficult, this is also something that can be delegated to a freelancer.

-Traffic: Once everything's been set up and running, the last frontier is to make more people aware of your product page on FBA and bring them to your product page. You can do this a myriad number of ways both free and pay. Your free options are social media and word-of-mouth while paid advertisements can be done on Facebook and other websites.

Product is Everything

Selling the right product is the single most critical factor for succeeding on FBA. These are usually cheaper, easily shipped products with minimal risks associated with transport. Your products should be known far and wide as goods which arrive fast and in the promised condition. This is harder to achieve with certain kinds of products, so be mindful of what you want to get into, especially in the beginning! So what are the things to consider to arrive at the "right" product? These include, among others:

-Price: Ideally, the products should be within the $10 to $50 range. This type of product sells the most and is the easiest to sell. This range is pretty much always more or less a sure ticket to success, so naturally, it marks the right place to start your business.

-Weight: Your products must weigh as light as possible. Mostly in the interest of shipping, storing, etc., lighter products will cost you less in these areas. Cheaper logistics are not the only reason to go for light products, though. The less they weigh, the less likely they are to be fragile, so the possibility of any potential problems with transport is greatly reduced.

-Competition: Like anywhere else where selling takes place, FBA is a marketplace like any other when it comes to competition. Determine if you have any actual and potential product competition within the top 5,000 best seller rank or BSR in your product's primary category. Also, ensure that you don't have competition from branded names in your chosen niche or category as this is a very potent competition killer. It is always a good idea to stay away from the big fish, especially so if you're the new kid on the block. Overcrowded, monopolized or otherwise full markets or niches are another things to avoid.

Another aspect of the competition you must check out is the reviews. The more reviews they have, especially positive ones, the greater is the competition and consequently, the challenge of breaking into the market. If the reviews on competing products are less than 50, it indicates a pretty good chance of cracking that niche or market.

-Toughness: Whenever possible, sell products that don't easily break. This will minimize your risks for refunds or replacements, both of which can significantly affect your margins. Consider the distances your goods might have to travel to get to the customer, as well as the means of transport required. Always calculate the risk involved in dealing with certain products, as some of them are a nightmare to ship. The smoother the shipping is, the more solid your base of income will become.

-Margins: Ideally, your margin (percentage of profit over selling price) must be at least 75% to make it worth your while. Always keep an eye on the numbers, this is the lifeblood of your business.

Success on FBA

The top sellers on Amazon are outliers, i.e., way different and separate from the rest of the pack. They tend to adopt the thinking that selling on Amazon is akin to the stock market or currencies trading. More than that, the following factors have - to a great extent - accounted for their success, if you apply these traits to your FBA game, then your chances of success are greatly increased :

-Economies of Scale: Selling more quantity of a product is more cost efficient — and profitable — compared to selling few. Selling on Amazon makes economies of scale much easier as the logistics are handled by a leading logistics behemoth. This is why smaller price ranges are a highway to success on FBA, and I stress 'highway'! Once your system is up and running, these products will sell fast and in large volumes. And in the process of getting up and running, well, obviously it's easier to amass a customer base through cheap and numerous products.

-Objectivity: The ability and willingness to be accountable for errors in judgment and adjusting accordingly is key to being flexible and successful in the arena that's called Amazon. The opposite just makes it impossible for sellers to do the right things at the right time for selling success on Amazon. Not everything goes according to plan all the time. This is completely normal. The trick is to learn from your mistakes, be responsible and keep going. Perhaps most importantly, you must have the ability to self-criticize and see the errors of your ways clearly and on your own. These virtues will help you understand when and how to adapt and improve your business, and this is crucial to success.

-Discipline: The most successful sellers are disciplined enough to control their inventories, cash flows and risk very well. If you are taking care of business personally, it is important to be meticulous and well organized. Think of it as managing a store, which is exactly what you're doing essentially.

-Focus: Maintaining a clear focus on your goal and having stone-hard will and determination. This is how we get places in life, and it's no different on FBA. The top Amazon sellers don't care about being right or wrong — they just care about making money. Lots of it!

-Time Frame: The most successful sellers view things from longer time frames such as quarters or years instead of days or weeks only. Even in other walks of life and business, this is the way that the vast majority of successful people think. It shows that you are thinking big, are ambitious and see the big picture. This kind of perception of time also helps you look forward with great foresight, which is a great organizational skill.

According to my personal experience, success on FBA is more about trial and error than clear learning. You'll stumble and fall sometimes, but you've got to keep going, that's how you'll learn in this marketplace. My top recommendation to you would be to sell something that you yourself love, and use daily. If you hate your own product, you're not only scamming other people to an extent, but you will sell it lethargically, which would eventually lead to failure.

INCOME SOURCE NO.3:

NICHE WEBSITES

A niche website is one that's focused on a very particular target or term, normally referred to as "keywords", which are what search engines like Google and Bing use to help people look for stuff on the Internet. And for your online passive income purposes, it's best your niche website's keyword is one that's very particular, unique or focused.

But, why a niche website?

One reason you may want to put up a niche website for passive income purposes is that it's relatively practical, i.e., cheap, to get up and running. If you'd like to speed up the process, you can pay for services and products that can help you do that but generally speaking, the only compulsory cost involved is for getting a domain name and a web hosting account, which averages between $5 to $7 monthly according to your choice of host.

While it may take some time and lots of work to set up your niche site, it's not complicated at all. Its relative simplicity in terms of setting up is another good reason to get into niche website marketing.

Another good reason is the results timeline. While it's true that nothing will make you money overnight, it's much faster in terms of driving traffic and generating income, compared to blogging, which may take you months or even years to build up enough of an audience to make good money.

Lastly, niche website marketing is one of the most passive of passive online incomes. In fact, it's possible for you to reach a point wherein it can run on autopilot while it generates income for you, leaving you with more time for other stuff like life or putting up other niche websites.

Yes, it may take time and work but once it's up and running, you can just leave it be.

It would be irresponsible of me if I don't come clean about the other side of niche website marketing, i.e., why other people aren't drawn to it or shun it. First is that it's not a slot machine. As mentioned earlier, you will have to put in the time and effort, especially when it comes to setting up the website. Moreover, it's not going to generate instant income, contrary to what other naysayers would have you believe. Not only does it take time to set up your site and everything it needs to work, it'll also take time for Google to actually notice your content, rank your website in search results for its niche keywords and for meaningful traffic to come to your site.

While you can earn a good income from niche website marketing, it's one that may be quite limited. The giveaway here is the word "niche", which means position and implies a high degree of specialization or focus. As such, you have less prospects compared to more generalized products that have much larger markets. While it's certainly possible for you to turn your niche site into one that's an authority on your particular niche, the chances are pretty low and eventually, your income potential can plateau. You can mitigate this risk by setting up other niche websites, which you can do with the amount of free time that you may enjoy once your niche website's already up and running.

Setting up your Niche Website

Like I wrote earlier, setting up a niche website may be a bit time consuming and require some amount of work but it's relatively simple to do. Here's how you do it in 7 steps:

STEP 1:
Brainstorm for niche site ideas, writing down as many as you can think of. Preferably, these should be in line with what you're passionate about. However, don't cling to a particular idea just because it is a passion of yours. You must be able to be objective and analytical, make double sure that your ideas are economically feasible i.e. popular. Working within a field you are passionate about does have many advantages, though.

STEP 2:
Once you've generated a pool of ideas, filter or narrow them down using the following set of criteria:

-Are there any products that you can discuss and review? The number of products you can post about is essential to your niche site taking off. The more products there are in a particular niche, the wider the scope of content you can produce for your visitors.

-Are there good affiliate programs that can provide potentially good commission income for you? Always keep an eye out for opportunities like affiliate programs, in marketing or whatever, these work wonders for many niche websites.

-Are existing niche website marketers actually making money off it? Of course, taking note of others' experiences is always a great way of improving your game and understanding what to change and what to keep. If you are unsure about taking a certain step along your way, the chances are that someone else already tried it, so learn from their failure or success.

-Are you able to generate around 100 articles on your niche or topic? Try to think up as many as possible to get an idea of how fruitful the niche you chose really is. If producing around 100 is a struggle, then perhaps your niche is too limited and should be replaced, or at least modified.

Now set up your website and begin generating your website's content using this outline:

-Write 5 review articles, one each for the 5 most popular products for your niche;

-Write 3 very detailed and easy to understand tutorials on your particular market or niche (how-to videos);

-Create 3 list posts; and

-Do it all over again.

1. Join affiliate-marketing programs that are related to your market or niche. Individual manufacturers or retailers dealing with products related to your particular niche might want to pay good money to advertise on your website. The chances of getting a serious affiliate marketing deal drastically increase as your following grows.

2. Research on the top 5 to 10 keywords or products to rank for. Strategically use the most popular keywords in your content and you greatly improve your search ranking over time. This is one of the ways to gradually get closer to the top of the search results.

3. Use Yoast SEO (Search Engine Optimization) specifically for WordPress and perform your niche website SEO for all pages and posts.

4. Email all your friends and social media contacts to spread the word about your niche website.

Ask your friends to share it as well and send it further.

5. Sign up for social media accounts for your niche website, e.g., Facebook, Twitter, Instagram and Pinterest. Having pages on such websites will help gather and group up your followers more effectively. You can also use your pages for newsletters, sharing ideas and content, attracting more followers, getting useful feedback, etc. Essentially, social media pages will do for your website what they do for individual people — immensely facilitate communication.

6. Sign up for a HARO (Help A Reporter Out) account. HARO is a service available online that helps journalists obtain feedback, public feedback, allowing them to link up with experts in particular issues to help them report on topics much better. Since you'll need to generate very good and accurate content like journalists do, a HARO account will be very helpful for you.

7. Identify and list all the major syndicated publications and blogs you'd like to be featured in for good exposure and promotions. Obtaining a spotlight for your niche website in a well-known publication may take you to whole new lengths of fame. If the said publication is focused closely on the same niche, that's even better because the feature will also be a valuable vouch for your site.

8. Begin to get in touch with blogs and websites on your niche that offer guest story ideas or posts. Another way to promote and get promoted, guest stories, posts, and appearances are a useful way of cooperation between websites and blogs in the same field.

9. Create a high-quality email series or content that you can give away for free in exchange for people's email addresses. Establishing an email list, through these and other means is a handy form of networking as well.

Finding your Niche

Earlier, we mentioned that the first thing you'll need to do before even setting up the actual website is to find your niche. Failure to do so may render all your hard work of setting up your site and promoting it useless or wasted because you may end up going for an unprofitable niche.

If you want to successfully find a good niche, you'll need to approach it like writing a blog, one where you'll need to generate a lot of good topics and content for. And as with Amazon FBA earlier, I highly recommend prioritizing niches that you're very familiar with or are passionate about. Why? Chances are, you're already knowledgeable on it. Just take note that what I mean by prioritizing is putting it first in terms of studying for profitability and not necessarily going for it. It's certainly possible that what you're passionate and knowledgeable about — say, dung beetles — isn't a profitable niche while classic cars — which you may not be passionate about as of the moment — is a profitable one. In which case, go for the classic cars niche. Prioritizing your passions and interest simply means that given your lack of knowledge on your identified potential niches' profitability, evaluate that of the one you're interested in or are passionate about first.

If you find that your ideal niche isn't profitable enough, don't be afraid to go with those that you're not yet knowledgeable about. Take time to read about it and familiarize yourself with it. Once you have enough basic knowledge, you can either research more stuff about it to create enough meaningful content or outsource it to freelance writers. There's more than one way to skin a, well, potato.

The truth is, with the ocean of knowledge that is the Internet, you can become well versed in practically any topic you can think of. Some will take more time to study thoroughly than others, but it can be done nonetheless. Once upon a primitive time, if an individual wanted to become knowledgeable about something, it was either formal education or hundreds, or even thousands, of hours in the library. The current state of affairs is such that you can learn and, subsequently, make money off your knowledge from a single place — your chair.

Surely, you can't expect to operate surgically on human brains without formal education and training, but when it comes to information, the Internet is limitless. So if a niche you want to get involved in lies beyond your expertise, get to learning and researching. Think of it as taking a course of sorts in order to get a job.

When you have laid out all of the prospects and ideas, all that's left is making the right choice. Now, there are a number of ways to go about this, but it begins with you having a firm understanding of how far your knowledge stretches in certain areas, your capacities to produce content, etc. It also makes the choice easier to have a clear notion of where exactly you want to take your website and what it is that you are hoping to achieve. One of the ways you can filter or short-list your niche ideas is through the margin-volume criteria. Entrepreneurs can be classified as those that prefer selling high-price-low-volume (high margin) products or low-price-high-volume (low margin) products. Each has their own sets of advantages and disadvantages. Those with high prices can give you significantly greater profit margins or spreads per unit of sale but because they're expensive, you'll need to sell less. In contrast, low priced products give you significantly fewer margins and require you to sell more units to generate the same amount of income as selling higher priced products. Which is better?

It's all up to you, depending on the pros and cons of each as it relates to the niche, the products, and the market.

Another filter through which you can narrow down your list of potential niches is the ability to write tons of articles or good content on the niche. A good benchmark — however arbitrary — is 50 articles to 100 articles. If you see yourself as being able to generate that much content over the course of the year, it means you're interested in or passionate about the niche and as such, are knowledgeable about it. This tells you that you'll probably have enough energy and interest to successfully see this through. If you can't, consider hiring ghost-writers, which of course will cost you more.

Given that hiring freelancers is an expense, and thus an investor's course of action, you may want to avoid doing so at first. It is probably best to put in the extra effort and produce as much of your own content as possible in the beginning. This way you will gather the maximum amount of capital, with which you can later hire help. At that point, you will begin to put the operation on autopilot.

Knowing if the niche has affiliate marketing programs that pay good commissions is another key factor to consider when narrowing down your list of niche ideas. While there are affiliate marketing programs for just about anything, what separates the great ones from the laggards are commissions. A good rule of thumb is to go for programs that offer at least a 10% commission.

Personally, I aim for around 20% to 35% commission. It may be difficult to find and set up the most profitable programs at first, of course, but you should definitely set the bar to 10% at the very least. These standards aren't merely about cashing in as quickly as possible, but also about presenting your website as an ambitious project instead of a cheap, small-time hobby. Keep in mind that digital products tend to give out higher commissions compared to physical products for one simple reason — cost. Digital products can be easily replicated at very little to no cost at all while physical products entail costs to reproduce. So if you're gunning purely for huge commissions, digital products may be best for you. Not to say that physical products suck at commissions. I'm just saying that while they can pay good commissions, they're not as high as those given to sellers of digital products.

More than just good commissions, you'll also want to find out if a particular niche is one where people actually make money. What good are sky-high commissions on niches with nary any customers? Maybe that's why they're offering high commissions — they're very hard to sell! As is the case with most things in life, if it appears as being too good to be true, then it probably isn't, true that is. With all the effort that goes into setting up your site, you do not want to throw it all away in a worthless market!

So how can you actually know if people actually make money in this niche? Here's how you can do it.

First, generate up to 10 keywords that you think people will use in search engines when searching for your product. If it's fat burners, particularly Hydroxycut, people may use the keywords

Hydroxycut Hardcore, Hydroxycut Elite or Hydroxycut reviews, among others.

Next, run these keywords through Market Samurai or Google's Keyword Tool in order to find out just how much traffic these keywords get. More than just discovering how many searches these keywords get monthly, you'll also get to discover other good keywords on your niche or product that you may not have thought of yet.

Now conduct a search on those keywords that generate tons of traffic and note if there are common websites that appear on the first pages of their search results. If there are, check them out. If there are no common ones, simply check out those top ranking sites per keyword search.

How can you tell if they're making money? Some sites actually divulge that they do, say like the website Kenrockwell.com, wherein he says at the bottom of every page that the website helps him support his family. But most other websites don't do that so how can you get an idea of whether they're making good money or not?

Market reviews are another way of doing so. If a niche has many product reviews with affiliate links in them, it's a good sign that maybe people are making decent money in the niche. Keep in mind that, while a vibrant market does mean that chances are there's money to be made there, it may also mean fierce competition.

Overall, you can get an idea if people are making money in a particular niche by looking at

keyword search traffic, reviews with affiliate links, high priced products, high commission rates.

Making Money through your Niche Website

There are several ways you can actually make money from your niche website, which include direct selling, paid links, paid advertisements, AdSense advertisements, and affiliate marketing. In the next chapter, we'll take a look into the world of affiliate marketing in detail.

On one final note concerning niche websites, although they require significant work to get things up and running smoothly, and entail more risk than is the case with passive income systems in general, they are still at the very top when it comes to passive income potential. Well-established websites that draw in significant amounts of traffic are among the most autonomous passive income endeavors. If a website manages to form a community around it, it is likely that this community might all but take over most of the functions of the website. Some of the more beloved sites routinely have users gladly assume the roles of administration, sometimes even for free! So if you know what you are doing and set everything up accordingly, this is an opportunity to create an almost living, moneymaking machine.

INCOME SOURCE NO.4:

DIVIDEND INVESTING

One of the options you may want to consider for making a passive income is dividend investing. This is a particular strategy for making money that is based on building up a nice collection of stocks that are considered safe. These stocks are not only safe, they are also ones that you will be able to make a considerable amount of money on through the whole year. Those who do this kind of investing in a wise way will see a lot of cash go into their accounts each month on regular basis.

You will get the money from these dividends based on how much the company which issued them makes. They will take from their profits and pay back the shareholders based on the amount that you have purchased of the company. The company will usually not disperse all of their profits.

They might put half back into the company for uses like advertising, expanding, or other projects to make more money and then give the other half to their shareholders.

This is a great way to make a passive income because you really do not have to put in much work other than handing over some money to the company. But there is a reason that not everyone will do this; there is a high risk involved and you could easily lose all of the money and more than you put into the company if you do not choose wisely and are not paying attention to the economy and the company you purchased from. If you make smart decisions and pay attention to what you are doing, this is a good way to make a lot of money without having to do as much work. Just remember, high payouts mean high risks, and you could easily lose out more with this method than when compared with some of the other options explored in this guidebook.

You need to be a smart consumer when it comes to doing dividends. Many people fall into the trap of just purchasing the stock that has the highest dividend because they think that they will make the most money with this idea. While that might make sense on paper, you really need to do your research. Often the companies that are offering really high dividends are the ones that are having problems. For example, the business that is offering the dividend might have a ratio of paying out that is so high that it is threatening future growth, so you will lose money in the future, or a ratio of debt to equity that is so high that the company is going to sink, taking your money with it. It does not matter how high the dividend is if the company goes under and you do not make any money.

There are a few things that dividend investors should think about in order to determine if they are a good investment or if the stock is going to be a waste of their time. Some of the things that you should consider include:

High dividend yield— although I just warned against investing in companies with too high a dividend yield, it is worth trying out a few with higher yields because they can be useful ways to make more money. There are plenty of reputable companies who will offer you a good investment if you give them a chance. Just make sure to do your research to ensure that you are making the right decision. Look for stocks that have a dividend that is higher than the interest you will make on treasury bonds through the United States government, to make it worth your time.

High dividend coverage— this is a process that you can use in order to determine if a dividend is actually safe for you to make money from or if there is some danger of you getting cut. You can ask yourself a few questions to figure out how safe a particular investment is. Ask if the business earns their money from a large pool of businesses or does it all come from just one business? If it's the latter, this could mean that your money could be harmed if something happens to that one business. You should also ask how much of the company's profit is paid out to you and how much they are investing in themselves or putting back. It is a general rule that the number of profits paid should not be more than 60 percent.

Qualified dividends— you will need to be aware of how the stock you are purchasing will be taxed, or you could lose money. Those who are just in it for the profit and quickly buy and sell stocks will find that they can be taxed pretty heavily. The government is looking for investors who will stay in the market for a long time so they tax less on those who remain in the market and more on those who are making a large profit by going through stocks like crazy.

You can sometimes find stocks that will be taxed less by the government if you stick with them, which means more money in your pocket.

Basically, dividend investing is an excellent opportunity if you are looking for a way to make some good money either on the side or in place of your current job. It is important that you are careful with which companies you invest in. Your profits are going to be tied to the company, so the more money they make, the more you will make, but it also works in reverse, and you can lose out by quite a bit. Doing your research and understanding the market and its trends can help you to make the right decision for your needs and to make some money from this strategy.

INCOME SOURCE NO.5:

PEER-TO-PEER LENDING

Last on my list of best sources of passive income is peer-to-peer lending. P2P lending is the practice of loaning money to borrowers who typically don't qualify for traditional loans. As the lender, you have the ability to choose the borrowers and are able to spread your investment amount out to mitigate your risk. This kind of lending will often take place online through various companies who will set it all up. Many of these companies will offer different platforms for lending, as well as ways to check the credit of those you are lending too. This works because you can lend money to someone who needs it but who may not be able to afford to get lending through other forms and you will make money on the interest that they pay back to you.

Some common characteristics of P2P lending are:

-It is done so that the lender can make money.

-There does not have to be a relationship between the borrowers and lenders before the process happens.

-There is usually a lending company available for help if needed.

-The transactions will occur online.

-Lenders will be able to choose who they will lend to.

-The loans will be unsecured, and there is no protection from the government.

-The loans are securities, which can be purchased by other lenders.

Essentially, you become a borrower's alternative to a bank loan. And these borrowers will be your sources of passive income.

By far, this is the most financial-minded option on our list of passive income ideas. You will need to have enough money to do the initial lending. This is a great way to make some extra money because you will not have to do as much work day-to-day. You will need to make sure to do your research though; if the other person skips out on the loan and does not pay you, it is your own fault and you are out of the money since there is no protection from the government. But if you do your research and find the right person, you can end up making a good profit from this method.

There are also some great advantages, but also some criticisms to do with this kind of lending investment. These would include some of the following:

Interest Rates

One of the biggest advantages for the borrowers is that the lending rates will be less than that at a bank. This is going to entice a lot of borrowers to the idea, which means that you could have a lot of potential for making money. The advantage for you as an investor is that there is a higher return possibility compared to other investments and from savings accounts.

Socially Conscious

This is a way for investors to not only make some good money but to help out others who are in need. This is a break-through for many borrowers because they are able to do the things that they want for prices that are lower than what is offered at the bank. You are giving these borrowers a break, and you are making money.

Credit Risk

Those who choose peer-to-peer lending have often been turned down by a bank or other option because of their credit scores. This is something that you will have to pay attention to because past performance is often indicative of future performance. If someone has not paid their bills in the past, who is to say that they are going to pay them in the future? When the borrower does not pay the money back, they end up being a huge risk to you because you will not be able to make any money. Take a look at past credit history and determine if it is a good idea to invest in a person and if you will get your money back.

Protection from the Government

Unlike banks and other lending institutions, you will not be getting protection from the government if the loan falls through. This means that all of the risks is on your shoulders, and if the person does not pay you back, you are left with no help at all.

While peer to peer lending is a good way to make some great money, you need to do so in a smart way. Do not just jump into the idea of thinking that you will make a ton of money in no time, because that is just not going to happen. You have to do your research and make smart investments in order to see the best returns.

P2P has its own fair share of risks and rewards, just as in other passive income sources, but know this: you will often have to make a certain amount of verified income (normally around $70,000 a year) before you are allowed to use these peer-to-peer passive income investments.

EPILOGUE

Thank you for reading this book, and I hope you've learned a lot about passive income, and have an idea of how you can make more money without breaking your back. However, knowing is only half the battle. The other half is putting into action what you have learned. The next step for you, after you finish this book, is to apply what you have learned, or if you want more information, find other sources and gather more knowledge about that particular topic. Keep learning and applying your knowledge, and you will eventually succeed in generating any amount of passive income you want. You have a long journey to cover, but if you take the first step now, years in the future you'll look back and thank yourself, but remember, take the first step now, not tomorrow, not at night, now.